DO IT LATER!

A 2016 Planner (or Non-Planner)

for the

Creative Procrastinator

by Mark Asher

Pomegranate

PORTLAND, OREGON

Item No. Y030

Pomegranate Communications, Inc.
19018 NE Portal Way, Portland OR 97230

Available in the UK and mainland Europe from Pomegranate Europe Ltd.
Unit 1, Heathcote Business Centre, Hurlbutt Road, Warwick, Warwickshire CV34 6TD, UK

© 2015 Mark Asher

Pomegranate publishes a wide variety of wall, mini wall, and desk calendars. Our extensive
line of paper gift products and books can be found at retail stores worldwide and online.
For more information or to place an order, please contact
Pomegranate Communications, Inc., 800 227 1428, www.pomegranate.com.

Designed by Carey Hall

Dates in color indicate US federal holidays.
Dates listed for all astronomical events in this calendar are based on Coordinated Universal Time (UTC),
the worldwide system of civil timekeeping. UTC is essentially equivalent to Greenwich Mean Time.
Moon phases and American, Canadian, and UK holidays are noted.
Jewish and Islamic holidays begin at sunset on the day preceding the date listed.
Dates of Islamic holidays are given for North America and are subject to adjustment.

 NEW MOON   FIRST QUARTER    FULL MOON   LAST QUARTER

Welcome, Procrastinator!

Tired of feeling out of step with the deadline-driven masses? Ready to turn over a new leaf but feeling a tad overwhelmed? Relax: you're among friends here. Let the drones of the world dart around with overloaded digital doodads and struggle with trendy time-management strategies. *Do It Later!* is designed for the way we time-indifferent people work. We're procrastinators—we get the important stuff done . . . when we get around to it. To be productive and creative, we first need to engage in critical activities, such as organizing our organizational strategies, staring out the window, creating the perfect playlist, and refilling our coffee. If you specialize in such delay tactics, or know someone who does, take a leisurely browse through the tips, activities, and wisdom sprinkled throughout this planner—for instance: "If there is no time like the present, why would I want to spend it working?" or "Surround yourself with enough doers and you'll never have to work a day in your life."

Then, start by writing a to-do item in a section that makes sense, such as "Things I have to do but that can wait a day, or two, or three . . . "; or "Small things I have to do before I can do the big things I have to do"; or "Things I absolutely have to do unless I absolutely don't want to do them." *Do It Later!* is filled with useful lists, such as "The Mind Is Like a Machine, and Every Machine Needs Maintenance" and "If You Can't Work, You Can Always Work up to Working." There's even a place to keep track of due dates and grace periods for your bills, a space to plan those crucial tax extensions, room to list contact information for procrastination partners, and weekly doodle blocks for that most beloved procrastination pastime.

Carry your new planner with pride. And if you never get around to starting the tasks you put in it—or even reading past this page—there's always tomorrow, or the day after, or . . .

—Mark Asher, fellow procrastinator

Procrastinator Wisdom

 Why do they call them "side projects" if I always end up working on them during the middle of the day?

Things I have to do but that can wait a day, or two, or three . . .

Small things I have to do before I can do the big things I have to do

Things I absolutely have to do unless I absolutely don't want to do them

Things people have been bugging me to do for a really long time

doodle block

Dec/Jan

BOXING DAY HOLIDAY (CANADA, UK) *monday*

28 362

tuesday

29 363

wednesday

30 364

thursday

31 365

NEW YEAR'S DAY *friday*

1 1

saturday

◐ **2** 2

January

s	m	t	w	t	f	s
					1	2
3	4	5	6	7	8	9
10	11	12	13	14	15	16
17	18	19	20	21	22	23
24	25	26	27	28	29	30
31						

sunday

3 3

Procrastinator Tip

Wait until the last minute to do something. It should only take you a minute to finish it.

Things I have to do but that can wait a day, or two, or three . . .

Small things I have to do before I can do the big things I have to do

Things I absolutely have to do unless I absolutely don't want to do them

Things people have been bugging me to do for a really long time

BANK HOLIDAY (SCOTLAND)

monday

4 ₄

tuesday

5 ₅

wednesday

6 ₆

thursday

7 ₇

friday

8 ₈

saturday

9 ₉

sunday

● **10** ₁₀

January

s	m	t	w	t	f	s
					1	2
3	4	5	6	7	8	9
10	11	12	13	14	15	16
17	18	19	20	21	22	23
24	25	26	27	28	29	30
31						

Procrastinator Wisdom

Hearing about the ills of procrastination is like reading the reasons not to skydive after you've left the plane.

Things I have to do but that can wait a day, or two, or three . . .

Small things I have to do before I can do the big things I have to do

Things I absolutely have to do unless I absolutely don't want to do them

Things people have been bugging me to do for a really long time

doodle block

January

monday

11 11

tuesday

12 12

wednesday

13 13

thursday

14 14

friday

15 15

saturday

 16 16

January

s	m	t	w	t	f	s
					1	2
3	4	5	6	7	8	9
10	11	12	13	14	15	16
17	18	19	20	21	22	23
24	25	26	27	28	29	30
31						

sunday

17 17

Procrastinator Activity

Type "procrastination cure" into an online search. Go through the top one thousand results and make a detailed list of cures to try someday.

Things I have to do but that can wait a day, or two, or three . . .

Small things I have to do before I can do the big things I have to do

Things I absolutely have to do unless I absolutely don't want to do them

Things people have been bugging me to do for a really long time

doodle block

January

MARTIN LUTHER KING JR. DAY	*monday*
	18 18
	tuesday
	19 19
	wednesday
	20 20
	thursday
	21 21
	friday
	22 22
	saturday
	23 23

January

s	m	t	w	t	f	s
					1	2
3	4	5	6	7	8	9
10	11	12	13	14	15	16
17	18	19	20	21	22	23
24	25	26	27	28	29	30
31						

sunday

○ **24** 24

Procrastinator Wisdom

 They say procrastinators are perfectionists. Well, I say better to be late and perfect than on time and average.

Things I have to do but that can wait a day, or two, or three . . .

Small things I have to do before I can do the big things I have to do

Things I absolutely have to do unless I absolutely don't want to do them

Things people have been bugging me to do for a really long time

doodle block

January

monday

25 25

tuesday

26 26

wednesday

27 27

thursday

28 28

friday

29 29

saturday

30 30

January

s	m	t	w	t	f	s
					1	2
3	4	5	6	7	8	9
10	11	12	13	14	15	16
17	18	19	20	21	22	23
24	25	26	27	28	29	30
31						

sunday

31 31

Procrastinator Tip

 WARNING: Tackling a difficult project after returning to work from a holiday weekend can cause dizziness, extreme resentment, and low self-esteem.

Things I have to do but that can wait a day, or two, or three . . .

Small things I have to do before I can do the big things I have to do

Things I absolutely have to do unless I absolutely don't want to do them

Things people have been bugging me to do for a really long time

doodle
block

February

monday

◗ **1** ₃₂

tuesday

2 ₃₃

wednesday

3 ₃₄

thursday

4 ₃₅

friday

5 ₃₆

saturday

6 ₃₇

February

s	m	t	w	t	f	s
		1	2	3	4	5	6
7	8	9	10	11	12	13
14	15	16	17	18	19	20
21	22	23	24	25	26	27
28	29					

sunday

7 ₃₈

Positive Descriptions of a Procrastinator (Written by a Procrastinator)

1. An extremely talented individual who thrives on the challenges of finding the most arduous ways to do things.

2. A sentimentalist who doesn't like to see things end.

3. A risk-taker who is not afraid to stop doing one thing to start doing something else.

4. An optimist who doesn't see the devil in the details but rather the details within the details.

5. A best friend who can be counted on to stop working to commiserate about your problems.

6. An adventurer who never discovers a detour unworthy of exploration.

7. A cautious individual who knows the value in assessing all options and opportunities before proceeding.

8. A curious explorer who translates a fork in the road into more forks in the road.

List 10 things you would do to make airplane travel enjoyable again.

1. _____

2. _____

3. _____

4. _____

5. _____

6. _____

7. _____

8. _____

9. _____

10. _____

Procrastinator Wisdom

 Rushing sex or a fine meal is never a good thing. How could work be any different?

Things I have to do but that can wait a day, or two, or three . . .

Small things I have to do before I can do the big things I have to do

Things I absolutely have to do unless I absolutely don't want to do them

Things people have been bugging me to do for a really long time

LUNAR NEW YEAR

monday

● **8** 39

MARDI GRAS

tuesday

9 40

ASH WEDNESDAY

wednesday

10 41

thursday

11 42

friday

12 43

saturday

13 44

February

s	m	t	w	t	f	s
	1	2	3	4	5	6
7	8	9	10	11	12	13
14	15	16	17	18	19	20
21	22	23	24	25	26	27
28	29					

VALENTINE'S DAY

sunday

14 45

Procrastinator Activity

My psychologist suggested that I time travel to a place in the future where I feel good about finishing a big project. Somehow I ended up on a beach with my feet in the sand and a drink in my hand.

Things I have to do but that can wait a day, or two, or three . . .

Small things I have to do before I can do the big things I have to do

Things I absolutely have to do unless I absolutely don't want to do them

Things people have been bugging me to do for a really long time

February

PRESIDENTS' DAY   *monday*
FAMILY DAY (CANADA, SOME PROVINCES)

◗ **15** 46

tuesday

16 47

wednesday

17 48

thursday

18 49

friday

19 50

saturday

20 51

February

s	m	t	w	t	f	s
	1	2	3	4	5	6
7	8	9	10	11	12	13
14	15	16	17	18	19	20
21	22	23	24	25	26	27
28	29					

sunday

21 52

Procrastinator Wisdom

 With deadlines looming, a thought like this will enter my head: can one procrastinate without being a procrastinator?

Things I have to do but that can wait a day, or two, or three . . .

Small things I have to do before I can do the big things I have to do

Things I absolutely have to do unless I absolutely don't want to do them

Things people have been bugging me to do for a really long time

doodle
block

February

tuesday

23 54

wednesday

24 55

thursday

25 56

friday

26 57

saturday

27 58

February

s	m	t	w	t	f	s
	1	2	3	4	5	6
7	8	9	10	11	12	13
14	15	16	17	18	19	20
21	22	23	24	25	26	27
28	29					

sunday

28 59

Procrastinator Tip

Postponement is the first step in acknowledging that something at hand needs to get done . . . eventually.

Things I have to do but that can wait a day, or two, or three . . .

Small things I have to do before I can do the big things I have to do

Things I absolutely have to do unless I absolutely don't want to do them

Things people have been bugging me to do for a really long time

monday

29 60

ST. DAVID'S DAY (WALES)   *tuesday*

◑ **1** 61

wednesday

2 62

thursday

3 63

friday

4 64

saturday

5 65

March

s	m	t	w	t	f	s
		1	2	3	4	5
6	7	8	9	10	11	12
13	14	15	16	17	18	19
20	21	22	23	24	25	26
27	28	29	30	31		

MOTHERING SUNDAY (UK)   *sunday*

6 66

Procrastinator Wisdom

You can't stop time, but you can slow it down by savoring it.

Things I have to do but that can wait a day, or two, or three . . .

Small things I have to do before I can do the big things I have to do

Things I absolutely have to do unless I absolutely don't want to do them

Things people have been bugging me to do for a really long time

March

INTERNATIONAL WOMEN'S DAY   *tuesday*

8 68

wednesday

● **9** 69

thursday

10 70

friday

11 71

saturday

12 72

March

s	m	t	w	t	f	s
		1	2	3	4	5
6	7	8	9	10	11	12
13	14	15	16	17	18	19
20	21	22	23	24	25	26
27	28	29	30	31		

DAYLIGHT SAVING TIME BEGINS   *sunday*

13 73

Luckily for Procrastinators, There Are Many Things that Need Tending

1. Keep your lawn sprinklers free of debris and spraying in the desired directions.

2. Clean the porches on your birdhouses. Don't have any birdhouses? Go buy a few and some birdseed. Then go to the bookstore and buy a book on birds.

3. Run tests to measure the cost savings and cleaning power of regular laundry detergent versus concentrated.

4. Read online reviews for antivirus and malware software. Then organize your bookmarks into subfolders.

5. Test your smoke and carbon monoxide detectors on a biweekly basis.

6. Become a master pruner and volunteer to trim all of your neighbors' shrubs and trees.

7. Start a rock collection, then catalog and photograph your gems.

8. Clearly label all of your tools with "Property of" followed by your full name and phone number.

9. Unclutter your car glove compartment, center console, and door pockets. Then make a written inventory of the contents.

10. Personalize your emergency kit by including a mix of your favorite songs, your favorite book, and some less-than-awful, non-perishable snacks.

If you could start a new country, list 10 national holidays you would instate.

1. _____

2. _____

3. _____

4. _____

5. _____

6. _____

7. _____

8. _____

9. _____

10. _____

Procrastinator Activity

Once I get around to it, I'm going to sue social media sites and smartphone manufacturers for causing me to procrastinate for prolonged periods of time, reducing my work output.

Things I have to do but that can wait a day, or two, or three . . .

Small things I have to do before I can do the big things I have to do

Things I absolutely have to do unless I absolutely don't want to do them

Things people have been bugging me to do for a really long time

doodle
block

March

monday

14 74

tuesday

◐ **15** 75

wednesday

16 76

ST. PATRICK'S DAY   *thursday*
BANK HOLIDAY (N. IRELAND)

17 77

friday

18 78

saturday

19 79

March

s	m	t	w	t	f	s
		1	2	3	4	5
6	7	8	9	10	11	12
13	14	15	16	17	18	19
20	21	22	23	24	25	26
27	28	29	30	31		

PALM SUNDAY   *sunday*
VERNAL EQUINOX 04:30 UTC

20 80

Procrastinator Wisdom

 Wouldn't it be great if money were as easy to make as it is to spend?

Things I have to do but that can wait a day, or two, or three . . .

Small things I have to do before I can do the big things I have to do

Things I absolutely have to do unless I absolutely don't want to do them

Things people have been bugging me to do for a really long time

doodle
block

monday

21 81

tuesday

22 82

wednesday

○ **23** 83

PURIM   *thursday*

24 84

GOOD FRIDAY   *friday*

BANK HOLIDAY (CANADA, UK)

25 85

saturday

26 86

March

s	m	t	w	t	f	s
		1	2	3	4	5
6	7	8	9	10	11	12
13	14	15	16	17	18	19
20	21	22	23	24	25	26
27	28	29	30	31		

EASTER   *sunday*

SUMMER TIME BEGINS (UK)

27 87

Procrastinator Tip

If you feel guilty at the end of the day about doing nothing, you have procrastinated improperly. Begin again tomorrow with a better attitude.

Things I have to do but that can wait a day, or two, or three . . .

Small things I have to do before I can do the big things I have to do

Things I absolutely have to do unless I absolutely don't want to do them

Things people have been bugging me to do for a really long time

doodle
block

EASTER MONDAY (CANADA, *monday*
UK EXCEPT SCOTLAND)

28 88

tuesday

29 89

wednesday

30 90

thursday

◑ **31** 91

friday

1 92

saturday

2 93

April

s	m	t	w	t	f	s
					1	2
3	4	5	6	7	8	9
10	11	12	13	14	15	16
17	18	19	20	21	22	23
24	25	26	27	28	29	30

sunday

3 94

Procrastinator Tip

 Life is fragile—make your bucket list your to-do list.

Things I have to do but that can wait a day, or two, or three . . .

Small things I have to do before I can do the big things I have to do

Things I absolutely have to do unless I absolutely don't want to do them

Things people have been bugging me to do for a really long time

doodle block

April

monday

4 95

tuesday

5 96

wednesday

6 97

thursday

● **7** 98

friday

8 99

saturday

9 100

sunday

10 101

April

s	m	t	w	t	f	s
					1	2
3	4	5	6	7	8	9
10	11	12	13	14	15	16
17	18	19	20	21	22	23
24	25	26	27	28	29	30

Procrastinator Activity

When stress strikes, close your eyes and jot down the first 10 things you picture. Then write a short poem that includes these words.

Things I have to do but that can wait a day, or two, or three . . .

Small things I have to do before I can do the big things I have to do

Things I absolutely have to do unless I absolutely don't want to do them

Things people have been bugging me to do for a really long time

doodle
block

April

monday

11 102

tuesday

12 103

wednesday

13 104

thursday

◗ **14** 105

friday

15 106

saturday

16 107

April

s	m	t	w	t	f	s
					1	2
3	4	5	6	7	8	9
10	11	12	13	14	15	16
17	18	19	20	21	22	23
24	25	26	27	28	29	30

sunday

17 108

Legitimate Reasons for *Not* Getting Things Done

1. I tried to tackle my procrastination and I pulled something.

2. For weeks I've been drowning in the sea of good intentions, and now I'm totally exhausted.

3. My Give-a-Damn Meter won't respond no matter how many times I hit it.

4. I need to focus on finding a new mouthwash and toothpaste combination.

5. It's Elvis's birthday and, to celebrate, I'm wearing a white sequined pantsuit, watching *Viva Las Vegas*, and eating peanut butter, bacon, and banana sandwiches.

6. My doctor has informed me that I am critically deficient in vitamin D, and it's imperative that I spend the day outside.

7. I parked my car in the alley behind my building last night, and I'm too scared to go back there this morning.

8. My garden is at a crisis stage and will die without my help.

List 10 celebrities you'd like (or not like) to be and why.

1. _____

2. _____

3. _____

4. _____

5. _____

6. _____

7. _____

8. _____

9. _____

10. _____

Procrastinator Wisdom

If God wanted models of efficiency, He would have created robots instead of humans.

Things I have to do but that can wait a day, or two, or three . . .

Small things I have to do before I can do the big things I have to do

Things I absolutely have to do unless I absolutely don't want to do them

Things people have been bugging me to do for a really long time

doodle
block

April

monday

18 109

tuesday

19 110

wednesday

20 111

thursday

21 112

EARTH DAY   *friday*

○ **22** 113

PASSOVER BEGINS   *saturday*
ST. GEORGE'S DAY (ENGLAND)

23 114

April

s	m	t	w	t	f	s
					1	2
3	4	5	6	7	8	9
10	11	12	13	14	15	16
17	18	19	20	21	22	23
24	25	26	27	28	29	30

sunday

24 115

Procrastinator Tip

 If you search "psychology of procrastination" online, you'll notice a lot of experts have too much time on their hands.

Things I have to do but that can wait a day, or two, or three . . .

Small things I have to do before I can do the big things I have to do

Things I absolutely have to do unless I absolutely don't want to do them

Things people have been bugging me to do for a really long time

doodle
block

Apr / May

monday

25 116

tuesday

26 117

wednesday

27 118

thursday

28 119

friday

29 120

saturday

◑ **30** 121

May

s	m	t	w	t	f	s
1	2	3	4	5	6	7
8	9	10	11	12	13	14
15	16	17	18	19	20	21
22	23	24	25	26	27	28
29	30	31				

sunday

1 122

Procrastinator Wisdom

"Killing time" sounds so violent. It's actually rather peaceful and enjoyable.

Things I have to do but that can wait a day, or two, or three . . .

Small things I have to do before I can do the big things I have to do

Things I absolutely have to do unless I absolutely don't want to do them

Things people have been bugging me to do for a really long time

BANK HOLIDAY (UK)   *monday*

2 123

tuesday

3 124

wednesday

4 125

CINCO DE MAYO   *thursday*

5 126

friday

● **6** 127

saturday

7 128

May

s	m	t	w	t	f	s
1	2	3	4	5	6	7
8	9	10	11	12	13	14
15	16	17	18	19	20	21
22	23	24	25	26	27	28
29	30	31				

MOTHER'S DAY   *sunday*

8 129

Procrastinator Tip

 Surround yourself with enough doers and you'll never have to work a day in your life.

Things I have to do but that can wait a day, or two, or three . . .

Small things I have to do before I can do the big things I have to do

Things I absolutely have to do unless I absolutely don't want to do them

Things people have been bugging me to do for a really long time

May

monday

9 130

tuesday

10 131

wednesday

11 132

thursday

12 133

friday

◑ **13** 134

saturday

14 135

sunday

15 136

May

s	m	t	w	t	f	s
1	2	3	4	5	6	7
8	9	10	11	12	13	14
15	16	17	18	19	20	21
22	23	24	25	26	27	28
29	30	31				

The Mind Is Like a Machine, and Every Machine Needs Maintenance

1. Before you begin working, sit in complete silence for one hour to calibrate your mind.

2. Begin each task slowly to allow your mind to warm up, reach its natural rhythm, and avoid any strains or sprains.

3. Take frequent snack breaks while working to keep your mind satiated and nimble.

4. Once you've successfully completed your entire to-do list, go outside for at least two hours to ventilate your mind.

5. Gradually resume working after each break by doing some light thinking about your next task. Carefully gather and organize the necessary materials.

6. Never occupy your mind with just work for long periods of time. Sporadically insert breaks for contemplation and play into your schedule to avoid cognitive exhaustion.

7. Engage in small, light-attention activities for the last two hours of the day to allow your fatigued mind to cool down.

8. At the end of your day, complete a series of mental stretches such as free associations, memorizing poetry, or completing one line of the *New York Times* crossword puzzle.

Come up with cute names for 10 different baby animals.

1. _____

2. _____

3. _____

4. _____

5. _____

6. _____

7. _____

8. _____

9. _____

10. _____

Procrastinator Activity

 Try this: have a crazy, frantic day where you complete everything on your task list, then have a mellow day where you do whatever you feel like doing. Which do you prefer?

Things I have to do but that can wait a day, or two, or three . . .

Small things I have to do before I can do the big things I have to do

Things I absolutely have to do unless I absolutely don't want to do them

Things people have been bugging me to do for a really long time

monday

16 137

tuesday

17 138

wednesday

18 139

thursday

19 140

friday

20 141

ARMED FORCES DAY

saturday

○ **21** 142

sunday

22 143

May

s	m	t	w	t	f	s
1	2	3	4	5	6	7
8	9	10	11	12	13	14
15	16	17	18	19	20	21
22	23	24	25	26	27	28
29	30	31				

Procrastinator Wisdom

If they can come up with ways to cure procrastination, certainly they can come up with ways to do nothing and still make money.

Things I have to do but that can wait a day, or two, or three . . .

Small things I have to do before I can do the big things I have to do

Things I absolutely have to do unless I absolutely don't want to do them

Things people have been bugging me to do for a really long time

doodle
block

May

VICTORIA DAY (CANADA)   *monday*

23 144

tuesday

24 145

wednesday

25 146

thursday

26 147

friday

27 148

saturday

28 149

May

s	m	t	w	t	f	s
1	2	3	4	5	6	7
8	9	10	11	12	13	14
15	16	17	18	19	20	21
22	23	24	25	26	27	28
29	30	31				

sunday

◗ **29** 150

Procrastinator Activity

Challenge yourself to join as many social media sites as possible in one workday. Create an elaborate spreadsheet of all their logins and passwords.

Things I have to do but that can wait a day, or two, or three . . .

Small things I have to do before I can do the big things I have to do

Things I absolutely have to do unless I absolutely don't want to do them

Things people have been bugging me to do for a really long time

MEMORIAL DAY
BANK HOLIDAY (UK)

monday

30 151

tuesday

31 152

wednesday

1 153

thursday

2 154

friday

3 155

saturday

4 156

June

s	m	t	w	t	f	s
			1	2	3	4
5	6	7	8	9	10	11
12	13	14	15	16	17	18
19	20	21	22	23	24	25
26	27	28	29	30		

sunday

 5 157

Procrastinator Tip

 Vividly imagining yourself jogging to the gym, then lifting weights for forty-five minutes, then doing cardio, and then jogging back home is healthy exercise for your mind.

Things I have to do but that can wait a day, or two, or three . . .

Small things I have to do before I can do the big things I have to do

Things I absolutely have to do unless I absolutely don't want to do them

Things people have been bugging me to do for a really long time

June

RAMADAN BEGINS   *monday*

6 158

tuesday

7 159

wednesday

8 160

thursday

9 161

friday

10 162

saturday

11 163

June

s	m	t	w	t	f	s
				1	2	3	4
5	6	7	8	9	10	11
12	13	14	15	16	17	18
19	20	21	22	23	24	25
26	27	28	29	30		

sunday

 12 164

Procrastinator Wisdom

 Going through college without procrastinating is like swimming without getting wet—it's not practical or desirable.

Things I have to do but that can wait a day, or two, or three . . .

Small things I have to do before I can do the big things I have to do

Things I absolutely have to do unless I absolutely don't want to do them

Things people have been bugging me to do for a really long time

doodle
block

June

monday

13 165

FLAG DAY · *tuesday*

14 166

wednesday

15 167

thursday

16 168

friday

17 169

saturday

18 170

June

s	m	t	w	t	f	s
				1	2	3	4
5	6	7	8	9	10	11
12	13	14	15	16	17	18
19	20	21	22	23	24	25
26	27	28	29	30		

FATHER'S DAY · *sunday*

19 171

If You Can't Work, You Can Always Work up to Working

1. Stare out the window and daydream about an upcoming project.

2. Reorganize your organizational systems and deep clean all your office furniture.

3. Walk around the office and talk to coworkers about their work.

4. Work *around* your work: research new routes to and from the office or rewrite a memo using synonyms for every word.

5. Watch a live stream of the International Space Station.

6. Add things to the top of your to-do list that you've already done. Cross them off.

7. Read a book in which one of the characters is a workaholic.

8. Spend a day around the water cooler or coffeemaker in a different office.

9. Think about a monumental task, such as the building of the first transcontinental highway.

10. Call a favorite former coworker and reminisce about a job well done.

List the first 10 things you would buy for your friends if you were given a million dollars.

1. _____

2. _____

3. _____

4. _____

5. _____

6. _____

7. _____

8. _____

9. _____

10. _____

Procrastinator Activity

 Type "positive procrastination" into an online search. Bask in the bounty of socially acceptable alternatives to doing work brought to you by your fellow procrastinators.

Things I have to do but that can wait a day, or two, or three . . .

Small things I have to do before I can do the big things I have to do

Things I absolutely have to do unless I absolutely don't want to do them

Things people have been bugging me to do for a really long time

June

SUMMER SOLSTICE 22:34 UTC

monday

○ **20** 172

tuesday

21 173

wednesday

22 174

thursday

23 175

friday

24 176

saturday

25 177

June

s	m	t	w	t	f	s
			1	2	3	4
5	6	7	8	9	10	11
12	13	14	15	16	17	18
19	20	21	22	23	24	25
26	27	28	29	30		

sunday

26 178

Procrastinator Wisdom

If there is no time like the present, why would I want to spend it working?

Things I have to do but that can wait a day, or two, or three . . .

Small things I have to do before I can do the big things I have to do

Things I absolutely have to do unless I absolutely don't want to do them

Things people have been bugging me to do for a really long time

monday

◑ **27** 179

tuesday

28 180

wednesday

29 181

thursday

30 182

CANADA DAY (CANADA)   *friday*

1 183

saturday

2 184

July

s	m	t	w	t	f	s
					1	2
3	4	5	6	7	8	9
10	11	12	13	14	15	16
17	18	19	20	21	22	23
24	25	26	27	28	29	30
31						

sunday

3 185

Procrastinator Tip

The older you get, the harder it is to make new friends. That's why it's a good idea to spend lots of time on Facebook communicating with the ones you have.

Things I have to do but that can wait a day, or two, or three . . .

Small things I have to do before I can do the big things I have to do

Things I absolutely have to do unless I absolutely don't want to do them

Things people have been bugging me to do for a really long time

 doodle block

INDEPENDENCE DAY | *monday*

● **4** 186

tuesday

5 187

EID AL-FITR | *wednesday*

6 188

thursday

7 189

friday

8 190

saturday

9 191

July

s	m	t	w	t	f	s
					1	2
3	4	5	6	7	8	9
10	11	12	13	14	15	16
17	18	19	20	21	22	23
24	25	26	27	28	29	30
31						

sunday

10 192

Procrastinator Wisdom

I read about the benefits of visualizing a task as being done. It didn't work for me—once I thought of the task as being done, I became elated and never got around to actually starting it.

Things I have to do but that can wait a day, or two, or three . . .

Small things I have to do before I can do the big things I have to do

Things I absolutely have to do unless I absolutely don't want to do them

Things people have been bugging me to do for a really long time

July

BANK HOLIDAY (N. IRELAND) *tuesday*

◑ **12** 194

wednesday

13 195

thursday

14 196

friday

15 197

saturday

16 198

July

s	m	t	w	t	f	s
					1	2
3	4	5	6	7	8	9
10	11	12	13	14	15	16
17	18	19	20	21	22	23
24	25	26	27	28	29	30
31						

sunday

17 199

Procrastinator Activity

If, by some strange circumstance, you happen to have a to-do list already made, insert "Take a break" after every third item.

Things I have to do but that can wait a day, or two, or three . . .

Small things I have to do before I can do the big things I have to do

Things I absolutely have to do unless I absolutely don't want to do them

Things people have been bugging me to do for a really long time

doodle
block

July

tuesday

○ **19** 201

wednesday

20 202

thursday

21 203

friday

22 204

saturday

23 205

July

s	m	t	w	t	f	s
					1	2
3	4	5	6	7	8	9
10	11	12	13	14	15	16
17	18	19	20	21	22	23
24	25	26	27	28	29	30
31						

sunday

24 206

Feeling Guilty About Procrastinating? Don't!

1. Resisting your heart's desire is the quickest way to starve your soul.

2. To demonstrate calm self-possession amidst obstacles or delays (even self-imposed ones) is called patience. Patience is so important that they made it a virtue.

3. Many great men and women throughout history have considered the landscape before tilling the soil.

4. Being gung ho may be valuable in war movies, but not so much in the day-to-day grind.

5. Slow-and-sure-footed beats quick-and-off-target every time.

6. When you look back on your life, the days of defiance are the ones you'll remember most.

7. Pets don't live as long as we do, so playing with them is never a waste of your time.

8. A two-hour luncheon with an elder is infinitely more important than putting in that same amount of time on an endless project.

9. Remember what poet Robert Frost said: "In three words I can sum up everything I've learned about life: It goes on."

List the first 10 things you'd like to accomplish after you retire (you can, of course, start planning now).

1. _____

2. _____

3. _____

4. _____

5. _____

6. _____

7. _____

8. _____

9. _____

10. _____

Procrastinator Tip

The experts and I agree: tackle small tasks first. Here's where we disagree: they believe this builds confidence and leads to the next item on your to-do list; I think it calls for a snack break or a nap.

Things I have to do but that can wait a day, or two, or three . . .

Small things I have to do before I can do the big things I have to do

Things I absolutely have to do unless I absolutely don't want to do them

Things people have been bugging me to do for a really long time

doodle
block

monday

25 207

tuesday

◐ **26** 208

wednesday

27 209

thursday

28 210

friday

29 211

saturday

30 212

sunday

31 213

July

s	m	t	w	t	f	s
					1	2
3	4	5	6	7	8	9
10	11	12	13	14	15	16
17	18	19	20	21	22	23
24	25	26	27	28	29	30
31						

Procrastinator Wisdom

Critics say being a productive procrastinator is sort of like being a rock that swims. They might have a point there.

Things I have to do but that can wait a day, or two, or three . . .

Small things I have to do before I can do the big things I have to do

Things I absolutely have to do unless I absolutely don't want to do them

Things people have been bugging me to do for a really long time

doodle
block

August

CIVIC HOLIDAY (CANADA, MOST PROVINCES)   *monday*
BANK HOLIDAY (SCOTLAND)

1 214

tuesday

● **2** 215

wednesday

3 216

thursday

4 217

friday

5 218

saturday

6 219

August

s	m	t	w	t	f	s
	1	2	3	4	5	6
7	8	9	10	11	12	13
14	15	16	17	18	19	20
21	22	23	24	25	26	27
28	29	30	31			

sunday

7 220

Procrastinator Wisdom

 Procrastination is what happens when dread meets anything that looks more pleasant.

Things I have to do but that can wait a day, or two, or three . . .

Small things I have to do before I can do the big things I have to do

Things I absolutely have to do unless I absolutely don't want to do them

Things people have been bugging me to do for a really long time

doodle
block

August

monday

8 ₂₂₁

tuesday

9 ₂₂₂

wednesday

◐ **10** ₂₂₃

thursday

11 ₂₂₄

friday

12 ₂₂₅

saturday

13 ₂₂₆

sunday

14 ₂₂₇

August

s	m	t	w	t	f	s
	1	2	3	4	5	6
7	8	9	10	11	12	13
14	15	16	17	18	19	20
21	22	23	24	25	26	27
28	29	30	31			

Procrastinator Activity

Using only emojicons, text elaborate murals to your friends.

Things I have to do but that can wait a day, or two, or three . . .

Small things I have to do before I can do the big things I have to do

Things I absolutely have to do unless I absolutely don't want to do them

Things people have been bugging me to do for a really long time

doodle
block

August

monday

15 ₂₂₈

tuesday

16 ₂₂₉

wednesday

17 ₂₃₀

thursday

○ ## 18 ₂₃₁

friday

19 ₂₃₂

saturday

20 ₂₃₃

August

s	m	t	w	t	f	s
		1	2	3	4	5	6
7	8	9	10	11	12	13
14	15	16	17	18	19	20
21	22	23	24	25	26	27
28	29	30	31			

sunday

21 ₂₃₄

How to Embrace Creative Chaos (while Not Getting Things Done)

1. Make a word cloud out of e-mails from your boss.

2. Create a detailed chart of all eclipses and meteor showers in your area. Design elaborate invitations to stargazing parties that you will never host.

3. Write a children's book about a dog or cat waiting to be adopted. Send the manuscript to every publisher you can think of.

4. Construct a window mosaic with Post-It notes.

5. Create an infographic comparing the condiments and their quantities in the company refrigerator and your home refrigerator.

6. Use the entire surface of the conference room whiteboard for a mural. Erase it the next day.

7. Make up a new language then compose a limerick about your job.

8. Create a conceptual art piece personifying your procrastination using only the contents of the office supply room or coworkers' wastebaskets.

List 10 things you miss about your favorite decade.

1. _____

2. _____

3. _____

4. _____

5. _____

6. _____

7. _____

8. _____

9. _____

10. _____

Procrastinator Tip

Scary things become less intimidating with repeat exposure. That's why I suggest looking at your workload several times before approaching it.

Things I have to do but that can wait a day, or two, or three . . .

Small things I have to do before I can do the big things I have to do

Things I absolutely have to do unless I absolutely don't want to do them

Things people have been bugging me to do for a really long time

doodle block

monday

22 235

tuesday

23 236

wednesday

24 237

thursday

◐ **25** 238

friday

26 239

saturday

27 240

August

s	m	t	w	t	f	s
	1	2	3	4	5	6
7	8	9	10	11	12	13
14	15	16	17	18	19	20
21	22	23	24	25	26	27
28	29	30	31			

sunday

28 241

Procrastinator Activity

 Organize the books on your bookshelf by color.

Things I have to do but that can wait a day, or two, or three . . .

Small things I have to do before I can do the big things I have to do

Things I absolutely have to do unless I absolutely don't want to do them

Things people have been bugging me to do for a really long time

doodle block

Aug / Sep

BANK HOLIDAY (UK EXCEPT SCOTLAND)	*monday*
	29 242
	tuesday
	30 243
	wednesday
	31 244
	thursday
	● **1** 245
	friday
	2 246
	saturday
	3 247
	sunday
	4 248

September

s	m	t	w	t	f	s
				1	2	3
4	5	6	7	8	9	10
11	12	13	14	15	16	17
18	19	20	21	22	23	24
25	26	27	28	29	30	

Procrastinator Wisdom

Some people may call it procrastinating, but I just call it waiting for all the information.

Things I have to do but that can wait a day, or two, or three . . .

Small things I have to do before I can do the big things I have to do

Things I absolutely have to do unless I absolutely don't want to do them

Things people have been bugging me to do for a really long time

doodle
block

September

September

s	m	t	w	t	f	s
				1	2	3
4	5	6	7	8	9	10
11	12	13	14	15	16	17
18	19	20	21	22	23	24
25	26	27	28	29	30	

LABOR DAY (US, CANADA)

monday

5 249

tuesday

6 250

wednesday

7 251

thursday

8 252

friday

◗ **9** 253

saturday

10 254

sunday

11 255

Procrastinator Tip

Learn to love your inner procrastinator. It makes a great accomplice for your inner child.

Things I have to do but that can wait a day, or two, or three . . .

Small things I have to do before I can do the big things I have to do

Things I absolutely have to do unless I absolutely don't want to do them

Things people have been bugging me to do for a really long time

doodle
block

September

EID AL-ADHA

monday

12 ₂₅₆

tuesday

13 ₂₅₇

wednesday

14 ₂₅₈

thursday

15 ₂₅₉

friday

○ **16** ₂₆₀

saturday

17 ₂₆₁

sunday

18 ₂₆₂

September

s	m	t	w	t	f	s
				1	2	3
4	5	6	7	8	9	10
11	12	13	14	15	16	17
18	19	20	21	22	23	24
25	26	27	28	29	30	

Procrastinator Activity

 I was hard at work when I noticed my dog. I got up and gave him a hug. Then I realized he needed a bath. So off we went to the groomer's. On the way, I decided we might as well go to the dog park and get super dirty first.

Things I have to do but that can wait a day, or two, or three . . .

Small things I have to do before I can do the big things I have to do

Things I absolutely have to do unless I absolutely don't want to do them

Things people have been bugging me to do for a really long time

September

monday

19 263

tuesday

20 264

INTERNATIONAL DAY OF PEACE   wednesday

21 265

AUTUMNAL EQUINOX 14:21 UTC   thursday

22 266

friday

◑ **23** 267

saturday

24 268

September

s	m	t	w	t	f	s
					1	2	3
4	5	6	7	8	9	10
11	12	13	14	15	16	17
18	19	20	21	22	23	24
25	26	27	28	29	30

sunday

25 269

The Psychology of Procrastination

1. Deadlines become less pressing and only mildly intimidating.

2. It feels as if your desire to work has suddenly abandoned your body.

3. The world, and your office supply drawer, begins to look incredibly disorganized and in need of immediate order.

4. When you try concentrating on work, you begin to smell salt air and hear waves crashing.

5. Visions of store sales fliers and coupons you've seen over the past few weeks pop into your head.

6. Cleaning tasks that seemed inane yesterday suddenly seem more pertinent and worth pursuing.

7. You start to smell recipes you've been thinking of trying.

8. Every time you try to go over your to-do list, you get lightheaded and then severely hungry.

9. Acute drowsiness sets in, much like being drugged, and an immediate and lengthy nap is the only cure.

Come up with 10 new names for crayon colors. Here's one to get you going: Rip-Roaring Red.

1. _____

2. _____

3. _____

4. _____

5. _____

6. _____

7. _____

8. _____

9. _____

10. _____

Procrastinator Activity

 Begin genealogical research on your family without using the Internet. Try to discover if you have a genetic predisposition to procrastination.

Things I have to do but that can wait a day, or two, or three . . .

Small things I have to do before I can do the big things I have to do

Things I absolutely have to do unless I absolutely don't want to do them

Things people have been bugging me to do for a really long time

Sep / Oct

monday

26 270

tuesday

27 271

wednesday

28 272

thursday

29 273

friday

30 274

saturday

● **1** 275

October

s	m	t	w	t	f	s
						1
2	3	4	5	6	7	8
9	10	11	12	13	14	15
16	17	18	19	20	21	22
23	24	25	26	27	28	29
30	31					

MUHARRAM

sunday

2 276

Procrastinator Wisdom

 People try to motivate me by saying, "Finish now and you'll have time for fun later." Sorry, but I belong to the "Life's uncertain, eat dessert first" crowd.

Things I have to do but that can wait a day, or two, or three . . .

Small things I have to do before I can do the big things I have to do

Things I absolutely have to do unless I absolutely don't want to do them

Things people have been bugging me to do for a really long time

October

ROSH HASHANAH

monday

3 277

tuesday

4 278

wednesday

5 279

thursday

6 280

friday

7 281

saturday

8 282

October

s	m	t	w	t	f	s
						1
2	3	4	5	6	7	8
9	10	11	12	13	14	15
16	17	18	19	20	21	22
23	24	25	26	27	28	29
30	31					

sunday

 9 283

Procrastinator Tip

Cyberslacking may be a serious deterrent to productivity, but it sure does pass the time quickly.

Things I have to do but that can wait a day, or two, or three . . .

Small things I have to do before I can do the big things I have to do

Things I absolutely have to do unless I absolutely don't want to do them

Things people have been bugging me to do for a really long time

doodle
block

October

COLUMBUS DAY   *monday*
THANKSGIVING DAY (CANADA)

10 284

ASHURA   *tuesday*

11 285

YOM KIPPUR   *wednesday*

12 286

thursday

13 287

friday

14 288

saturday

15 289

October

s	m	t	w	t	f	s
						1
2	3	4	5	6	7	8
9	10	11	12	13	14	15
16	17	18	19	20	21	22
23	24	25	26	27	28	29
30	31					

sunday

○ **16** 290

Procrastinator Activity

Pick two completely unrelated topics, such as hyperboles and tomatoes. Start an Internet search for one topic then attempt to navigate to the other topic by clicking on links.

Things I have to do but that can wait a day, or two, or three . . .

Small things I have to do before I can do the big things I have to do

Things I absolutely have to do unless I absolutely don't want to do them

Things people have been bugging me to do for a really long time

doodle
block

October

tuesday

18 292

wednesday

19 293

thursday

20 294

friday

21 295

saturday

◑ **22** 296

October

s	m	t	w	t	f	s
						1
2	3	4	5	6	7	8
9	10	11	12	13	14	15
16	17	18	19	20	21	22
23	24	25	26	27	28	29
30	31					

sunday

23 297

Procrastinator Wisdom

 If everything begins with nothing, isn't it best to start by doing nothing?

Things I have to do but that can wait a day, or two, or three . . .

Small things I have to do before I can do the big things I have to do

Things I absolutely have to do unless I absolutely don't want to do them

Things people have been bugging me to do for a really long time

October

UNITED NATIONS DAY

monday

24 298

tuesday

25 299

wednesday

26 300

thursday

27 301

friday

28 302

saturday

29 303

October

s	m	t	w	t	f	s
						1
2	3	4	5	6	7	8
9	10	11	12	13	14	15
16	17	18	19	20	21	22
23	24	25	26	27	28	29
30	31					

SUMMER TIME ENDS (UK)

sunday

● **30** 304

Perfectionism Is a Killer—
Don't Fall Prey to It!

1. Arrive to work at a slightly different time every day.

2. After you've created a new task list, close your eyes and point to a place on the paper or screen with your right index finger. Delete or move this item to the bottom of the list.

3. At some point during each day drift away to a place called Tomorrowland.

4. Experiment with turning your work in early and unchecked to break the nasty habit of perfectionism.

5. Set the clocks in your home, car, and office to different times.

6. Work with your feet on the desk and your head on a big fluffy pillow.

7. Allow yourself to engage in every whim, detour, or diversion that enters your mind.

8. Get a clear picture of your work deadlines in your head, then watch them slowly pass by.

Make a list of 10 state capitals. Give yourself bonus points for including state mottos.

1. _____

2. _____

3. _____

4. _____

5. _____

6. _____

7. _____

8. _____

9. _____

10. _____

Procrastinator Tip

 To each his own. For me playing Minecraft and talking on the phone at the same time is being productive.

Things I have to do but that can wait a day, or two, or three . . .

Small things I have to do before I can do the big things I have to do

Things I absolutely have to do unless I absolutely don't want to do them

Things people have been bugging me to do for a really long time

Oct / Nov

HALLOWEEN   *monday*

31 305

tuesday

1 306

wednesday

2 307

thursday

3 308

friday

4 309

saturday

5 310

November

s	m	t	w	t	f	s
		1	2	3	4	5
6	7	8	9	10	11	12
13	14	15	16	17	18	19
20	21	22	23	24	25	26
27	28	29	30			

DAYLIGHT SAVING TIME ENDS   *sunday*

6 311

Procrastinator Activity

 Plan an unprocrastination day.
You may never get around to it.

Things I have to do but that can wait a day, or two, or three . . .

Small things I have to do before I can do the big things I have to do

Things I absolutely have to do unless I absolutely don't want to do them

Things people have been bugging me to do for a really long time

doodle
block

November

monday

◐ **7** 312

ELECTION DAY   tuesday

8 313

wednesday

9 314

thursday

10 315

VETERANS DAY   friday
REMEMBRANCE DAY (CANADA)

11 316

saturday

12 317

November

s	m	t	w	t	f	s
		1	2	3	4	5
6	7	8	9	10	11	12
13	14	15	16	17	18	19
20	21	22	23	24	25	26
27	28	29	30			

sunday

13 318

Procrastinator Tip

 Every time I get ready to tackle an undesirable project, I get hungry. Then, after I eat, I get sleepy. When I get up, I'm hyper. That's usually when I call a friend and go out.

Things I have to do but that can wait a day, or two, or three . . .

Small things I have to do before I can do the big things I have to do

Things I absolutely have to do unless I absolutely don't want to do them

Things people have been bugging me to do for a really long time

doodle
block

November

monday

○ **14** 319

tuesday

15 320

wednesday

16 321

thursday

17 322

friday

18 323

saturday

19 324

sunday

20 325

November

s	m	t	w	t	f	s
		1	2	3	4	5
6	7	8	9	10	11	12
13	14	15	16	17	18	19
20	21	22	23	24	25	26
27	28	29	30			

Procrastinator Wisdom

 The "experts" say procrastinators lack self-discipline, but I'm extremely disciplined when it comes to choosing to do something pleasurable over something painful.

Things I have to do but that can wait a day, or two, or three . . .

Small things I have to do before I can do the big things I have to do

Things I absolutely have to do unless I absolutely don't want to do them

Things people have been bugging me to do for a really long time

November

monday

◑ **21** ₃₂₆

tuesday

22 ₃₂₇

wednesday

23 ₃₂₈

THANKSGIVING DAY · thursday

24 ₃₂₉

friday

25 ₃₃₀

saturday

26 ₃₃₁

sunday

27 ₃₃₂

November

s	m	t	w	t	f	s
		1	2	3	4	5
6	7	8	9	10	11	12
13	14	15	16	17	18	19
20	21	22	23	24	25	26
27	28	29	30			

Procrastinator Tip

 Be respectful of the rhythms of your mind by waiting for the right moment to begin a new project. Patience is key, as the process could take up to several weeks.

Things I have to do but that can wait a day, or two, or three . . .

Small things I have to do before I can do the big things I have to do

Things I absolutely have to do unless I absolutely don't want to do them

Things people have been bugging me to do for a really long time

monday

28 ₃₃₃

tuesday

● **29** ₃₃₄

ST. ANDREW'S DAY (SCOTLAND)   *wednesday*

30 ₃₃₅

thursday

1 ₃₃₆

friday

2 ₃₃₇

saturday

3 ₃₃₈

December

s	m	t	w	t	f	s
				1	2	3
4	5	6	7	8	9	10
11	12	13	14	15	16	17
18	19	20	21	22	23	24
25	26	27	28	29	30	31

sunday

4 ₃₃₉

My Dream Workspace Would Include . . .

1. A laundry room stocked with a large magazine selection and a state-of-the-art espresso machine.

2. An elliptical machine with a laptop tethered to it, so I could look like I'm working while I'm working out.

3. A cheerful area with a plethora of pillows for napping, brainstorming, and pillow fights.

4. Therapy dogs, cats, or goldfish stationed all around to reduce tension and increase joyfulness.

5. A vegetable garden on the roof, so you could watch something grow besides your to-do list.

6. A large gym with padded walls and a punching bag where you can let out frustration.

7. A pastry chef baking elaborate desserts and doughy delights.

8. Window shades displaying different artwork, so instead of looking at the side of a building or the street, you could see something interesting.

9. A kitchenette and a minibar in every office for those times when your brain needs nourishment or relaxation.

Come up with 10 middle names for your dog or cat.

1. _____

2. _____

3. _____

4. _____

5. _____

6. _____

7. _____

8. _____

9. _____

10. _____

Procrastinator Activity

 Write an acrostic poem using the letters in the word *procrastination.*

Things I have to do but that can wait a day, or two, or three . . .

Small things I have to do before I can do the big things I have to do

Things I absolutely have to do unless I absolutely don't want to do them

Things people have been bugging me to do for a really long time

doodle
block

December

monday

5 340

tuesday

6 341

wednesday

◑ **7** 342

thursday

8 343

friday

9 344

saturday

10 345

sunday

11 346

December

s	m	t	w	t	f	s
				1	2	3
4	5	6	7	8	9	10
11	12	13	14	15	16	17
18	19	20	21	22	23	24
25	26	27	28	29	30	31

Procrastinator Tip

The cost of waiting a little longer is always less than the dread of jumping into something you loathe doing.

Things I have to do but that can wait a day, or two, or three . . .

Small things I have to do before I can do the big things I have to do

Things I absolutely have to do unless I absolutely don't want to do them

Things people have been bugging me to do for a really long time

doodle
block

December

MAWLID AN-NABI   *monday*

12 347

tuesday

13 348

wednesday

○ **14** 349

thursday

15 350

friday

16 351

saturday

17 352

December

s	m	t	w	t	f	s
				1	2	3
4	5	6	7	8	9	10
11	12	13	14	15	16	17
18	19	20	21	22	23	24
25	26	27	28	29	30	31

sunday

18 353

Procrastinator Activity

 Want to make work more fun and less predictable? Try shuffling the order of your to-do items three times a day. If you don't like what you see, shuffle again until content.

Things I have to do but that can wait a day, or two, or three . . .

Small things I have to do before I can do the big things I have to do

Things I absolutely have to do unless I absolutely don't want to do them

Things people have been bugging me to do for a really long time

December

monday

19 354

tuesday

20 355

WINTER SOLSTICE 10:44 UTC

wednesday

◑ **21** 356

thursday

22 357

friday

23 358

saturday

24 359

December

s	m	t	w	t	f	s
				1	2	3
4	5	6	7	8	9	10
11	12	13	14	15	16	17
18	19	20	21	22	23	24
25	26	27	28	29	30	31

CHRISTMAS

HANUKKAH BEGINS

sunday

25 360

Procrastinator Tip

 In between sessions of procrastinating (or, if you must, working), it's important to take plenty of time to rest and eat right to enhance your recovery.

Things I have to do but that can wait a day, or two, or three . . .

Small things I have to do before I can do the big things I have to do

Things I absolutely have to do unless I absolutely don't want to do them

Things people have been bugging me to do for a really long time

doodle block

Dec / Jan 2017

CHRISTMAS HOLIDAY · *monday*
BOXING DAY (CANADA, UK)
KWANZAA BEGINS · **26** · 361

CHRISTMAS HOLIDAY (CANADA, UK) · *tuesday*

27 · 362

wednesday

28 · 363

thursday

● **29** · 364

friday

30 · 365

saturday

31 · 366

January

s	m	t	w	t	f	s
1	2	3	4	5	6	7
8	9	10	11	12	13	14
15	16	17	18	19	20	21
22	23	24	25	26	27	28
29	30	31				

NEW YEAR'S DAY · *sunday*

1 · 1

Sometimes You Just Need
Something to Pass the Time

1. Use Google Maps to see street views of famous places.

2. Find out what the price of milk was the year you were born.

3. Find the most obscure trivia question you can. Fact-check the answer.

4. Search online for old photos and videos of your parents' hometowns.

5. Use an online translator to learn how to say 10 words in 10 different languages.

6. Make a list of cool spots to visit during summer and hot places to visit in winter.

7. Perfect an accent.

8. Plan all of your friends' and relatives' birthday gifts for the next five years.

9. Organize the clothes you will wear for the next month.

10. Go to the toy store and buy something that makes you feel like a kid.

List 10 different time periods you would visit if you could time travel.

1. _____

2. _____

3. _____

4. _____

5. _____

6. _____

7. _____

8. _____

9. _____

10. _____

Procrastinator Activity

 Develop an elaborate 15-step process for refilling your coffee mug, complete with barista apron and espresso machine sound effects.

Things I have to do but that can wait a day, or two, or three . . .

Small things I have to do before I can do the big things I have to do

Things I absolutely have to do unless I absolutely don't want to do them

Things people have been bugging me to do for a really long time

doodle
block

January 2017

BANK HOLIDAY (SCOTLAND)   *tuesday*

3 3

wednesday

4 4

thursday

◗ **5** 5

friday

6 6

saturday

7 7

January

s	m	t	w	t	f	s
1	2	3	4	5	6	7
8	9	10	11	12	13	14
15	16	17	18	19	20	21
22	23	24	25	26	27	28
29	30	31				

sunday

8 8

Grace Periods for Bills Due &
Tax Extension Schedule/Plan

1. _____

2. _____

3. _____

4. _____

5. _____

6. _____

7. _____

8. _____

9. _____

10. _____

People to Call When You Don't Feel Like Working

NAME	MOBILE
	PHONE (H)
	PHONE (W)

NAME	MOBILE
	PHONE (H)
	PHONE (W)

NAME	MOBILE
	PHONE (H)
	PHONE (W)

NAME	MOBILE
	PHONE (H)
	PHONE (W)

2017

January

s	m	t	w	t	f	s
1	2	3	4	5	6	7
8	9	10	11	12	13	14
15	16	17	18	19	20	21
22	23	24	25	26	27	28
29	30	31				

February

s	m	t	w	t	f	s
			1	2	3	4
5	6	7	8	9	10	11
12	13	14	15	16	17	18
19	20	21	22	23	24	25
26	27	28				

March

s	m	t	w	t	f	s
			1	2	3	4
5	6	7	8	9	10	11
12	13	14	15	16	17	18
19	20	21	22	23	24	25
26	27	28	29	30	31	

April

s	m	t	w	t	f	s
						1
2	3	4	5	6	7	8
9	10	11	12	13	14	15
16	17	18	19	20	21	22
23	24	25	26	27	28	29
30						

May

s	m	t	w	t	f	s
	1	2	3	4	5	6
7	8	9	10	11	12	13
14	15	16	17	18	19	20
21	22	23	24	25	26	27
28	29	30	31			

June

s	m	t	w	t	f	s
				1	2	3
4	5	6	7	8	9	10
11	12	13	14	15	16	17
18	19	20	21	22	23	24
25	26	27	28	29	30	

July

s	m	t	w	t	f	s
						1
2	3	4	5	6	7	8
9	10	11	12	13	14	15
16	17	18	19	20	21	22
23	24	25	26	27	28	29
30	31					

August

s	m	t	w	t	f	s
		1	2	3	4	5
6	7	8	9	10	11	12
13	14	15	16	17	18	19
20	21	22	23	24	25	26
27	28	29	30	31		

September

s	m	t	w	t	f	s
					1	2
3	4	5	6	7	8	9
10	11	12	13	14	15	16
17	18	19	20	21	22	23
24	25	26	27	28	29	30

October

s	m	t	w	t	f	s
1	2	3	4	5	6	7
8	9	10	11	12	13	14
15	16	17	18	19	20	21
22	23	24	25	26	27	28
29	30	31				

November

s	m	t	w	t	f	s
			1	2	3	4
5	6	7	8	9	10	11
12	13	14	15	16	17	18
19	20	21	22	23	24	25
26	27	28	29	30		

December

s	m	t	w	t	f	s
					1	2
3	4	5	6	7	8	9
10	11	12	13	14	15	16
17	18	19	20	21	22	23
24	25	26	27	28	29	30
31						